Kaleidoscopic Soul

Codrina Ibanescu

Copyright © Codrina Ibanescu, 2020
All rights reserved.

To contact author: codrina.ibanescu@gmail.com

ISBN: 978-1-989403-21-1

Front and back cover images: Codrina Ibanescu

Design & Layout: ThePublishingMentor.com

Self-published through:
In Our Words Inc /inourwords2008@gmail.com

Contents

True Freedom 5
Gaspe 6
Homefree 7
Kindred Spirits 9
Soul Sisters 10
Untitled - Him/Her 11
The Westward Calling 12
A Time for Leaving 13
Carpe Noctum 15
Hope 16
Our Love 17
The Wrath of the Sea 18
Suffering 19
Shooting Star 21
Love 23
The Mystic Fruit 24
Soul Retrieval 25
Dancing on your Bones 26
Art 28
The Moon 29
I Hope That You Find What You are Looking For 31
Transfiguration 32
The Unravelling 33
Illuminated 35
Serendipity 36
Grandma's Girl 37
Moving Through 39

The Wild Self	41
Light	42
Libertas Perfundet Omnia Luce	43
You are my Sun	44
The Voice Within	45
Unconditional Love	46
Ode to Wild Woman	47
Stay Wild	48
Love Letters to the Universe	49
Solace	51
Infinite Possibilities	52
Paint	53
Acceptance	56
Ephemeral	57
Horizon	58
Letting Go	59
I Found, You	60
Meaningful Meanderings	61
Full Moon Risin'	63
Happiness	64
Acknowledgements	65

Libertas Perfundet Omnia Luce

"Freedom will flood all things with light."

True Freedom

- Ross Lake, British Columbia

If freedom had a face,
it would be the mountain and the sea,
you see.
There is no place I would rather be.

And if humility had a smile.
It would stretch out from mile to mile,
Hoping that once in a while.
It would reach a person to touch.

Kindness is a virtue,
but it isn't always shown,
Just as the wind between the trees.
When the western wind is blown.

When you live.
You don't need much,
And when you are in love.
You should show it as such…

Time does not stop for anyone.
You're the only one in a rush,
Life is as precious as the Soul behind your eyes.
And should be only moulded when lush.

Gaspe

Between the shoreline and the sea
Streaming endlessly
The misty clouds rest gently
Upon the evergreen

The empty horizon
Surrounds me
Gentle sounds and murmuring
Beside the shoreline and the sea

Homefree

- Lost Coast, California

Somewhere down that
Lonely road
You find peace.

Now you don't find it
In a person, place
Or even a thing—

It is you.
It has always been you,
And it becomes a part of you.

You begin to look back
And recall many moments
Realizing how beautiful they all were.

The little things
Begin to matter,
While the others wash away.

The tides of the ocean
And the sea itself
Remind you of how vast living is.

It is ever-changing
And yet something is the same,
But you just can't put a finger on it.

Travelling the road
Brings you to gratitude,
And most importantly forgiveness.

You begin to deconstruct yourself
And analyze, understanding who you are
From the core of your being.

It is a process of humbling,
Because in the end
There never was a 'you.'

You are like the moon
Which goes through phases
And still shines through the dark.

You are everything.
Every person you meet
And those you don't

You have the whole world
Ahead of you to explore,
But you are restless.

You want it all now… be patient.
The light takes time to reach
The darkest corners of a room.

Kindred Spirits

Your laugh,
Your eyes, withdrawn—
The memories
Come and gone

The subtle appreciation
The hugs held just too tight
Love and affection
In its purest form

Thank you for—
Your kindness,
I appreciate
Your truth

And though we are
But kindred spirits,
You mean so much
And I love you

Soul Sisters

- For Nadia

Graceful and insightful
You walk into the room
And illuminate our lives
Like the sun which chases the moon.

Gentle and bright,
Loyal and profound
I couldn't imagine my life
Without you around.

Your words of encouragement
Moments of insight,
Tender moments of laughter
Which make my days bright.

Graceful, mysterious and insightful
You walk into the room
And illuminate our lives
Like the sun which chases the moon

And when we deeply converse
You are someone who truly understands
The fragile nature of existence, friendship and love
And all of life's demands

You make my life bright,
I hope you take this to be true.
And no matter how far we may be
Know that I really love you.

Untitled - Him/Her

"God, you would have loved her.
The wind that brushed her hair,
the light on her face,
And in her eyes…
an entire Universe in disguise.

God, you would have loved her.
The way that her whole being lit up
When she was talking about what she loved,
And held dear.
The way compassion filled her heart,
For those far and near."

"God, you would have loved him.
The way that doubt filled his Soul
Anytime anyone complimented him,
Or made him feel whole.

God, you would have loved him.
The smile on his face,
How, for every single moment,
There was never any space—
between us.

God, you would have loved him,
The compassion in his Heart,
How he always wished to make others
Appreciated, loved, and heard."

The Westward Calling

God has chosen you
As if he must have known
That the western wind
Lays inside of you
Awaiting to be blown

A Time for Leaving

Deep inside
A fire roars
And it keeps the momentum
Going on

When you are
On the road
And you are
Travelling from place to place

You become a part of
This infinite
Rich
Adventurous flow

If the flame
Is left untamed
Or unfed
It begins to diminish

You experience
So much light
So much love
And loneliness

And once in a while
You look back and smile
Remembering that you too
Have a home

Momentarily
Your backpack
And the arms of your other
Become all you need

You nourish yourself
Through becoming a part
Of everything
And everyone you meet

But like each moment
And each person
That enters with delicate grace
There comes a time for leaving

The fire must burn once more
And without fuel
Without wind
It cannot thrive

You move on
Forward through the setting sun
Realizing that at the end of the day
You are always okay

Carpe Noctum

Artists look
At things differently—
Though it is
Important to know,
There is
A natural relationship
With the dark

Hope

And I learned early on
That the simple things
Were in fact
The ones worth living for

They do not teach you this
In school,
Or on television
No.
You learn one cold winter's night
As your toes and fingers freeze
But you enjoy yourself so much
That you forget everything

That is a feeling
That is brought upon the basis
Of purely living
And enjoying every damn minute of it
You cannot ask for this feeling
For it arrives on your doorstep
Unexpectedly one day

It gives you hope
And reminds you to keep going
No matter what.
To keep your spark aflame
No matter how small it may be
And to be grateful
For there is so much beauty
Still left
For eyes who choose to see it

Our Love

When I hear the sound
Of the waves crashing
Into the rock,
I will think of you, my dear.

And when I see
the sun arise
Into the vast star-streaked sky
I will wake to you, my dear

For tomorrow holds no yesterdays
And our embrace knows no past—
Hold me tight and believe
That these waves too will pass.

The Wrath of the Sea

Be gentle with me—
Just please, be gentle…
I ask
But instead he rocks the harbours
And makes it
So that I can never return

Suffering

I decided to write you a poem
To finally tell you the truth
That sometimes things happen
And you have no proof

That you can go through life
Questioning your faith
And wondering
The purpose of your being here.

I'm here to remind you
That things were not always great,
And that when you were a child
You still did feel the pain

And here I sit wondering
If there is really any gain
In spending my life wandering
From plain to plain

Dreamscape to darkness
Physically to light
And everything in between
The beating of my heart
And each breath I take

In life, you end up feeling loss
Like a sharp knife
There is no avoiding it
And so it makes you feel
Is there any real reason
In living at all?

Feeling so absent
And yet so present
Brings forth many feelings
And at the end of the day
I remain like a child
Who has run for far too long
And has lost her way

The forest has been leading me
Through for a long time
And it is as if every time
The light
Is present

Then it is gone again
Like a flash
Or the flicker of candlelight
In a dark hallway

The only thing left to do
Is to feel things entirely
To enter that space of grief
And let it become
The entirety of your being
To swallow your pride
And remember that in the end
Entropy rules all mortal flesh
And it is alright to not feel okay

Shooting Star

This aching in my chest that I know so well
Tears they fall
I cannot contain my feelings no longer
They leak out of me
Out of my skin
My eyes hold a vacant stare
Thoughts that I should not have are there
I am constantly reminding myself of my own existence
Scaring myself out of being
And for an instance I am a shell
Merely consciousness floating above myself
I am constantly putting others before myself
And still it is not enough
I feel inconsiderate
Full of shame
And what for?
There are too many things I want to do
Too many things that have already been done
I want to tear out this void I feel between my breasts
And throw it out into the sky
Where it will wander and eventually catch the eye of another
A shooting star, or perhaps the soul travelling
They would not know nor will they question
If it is a lingering sadness and hopelessness streaking across the sky
No
They will just gawk shake their heads and watch in wonder
But few will look up and know
They will understand this signal and send out one of their own
And they will collide to form a spectacle
All gaze at the naked helpless human attempting to be so great
And great I will be
As I will walk away a stronger woman than ever before
Understanding the understood

Through the eyes and lens of more than my own
As if there was a Polaroid to capture every moment
Every scenery that I have felt and seen
Ever changing
Ever being
Flesh and spirit

Love

I need to let go of fear.
God is around me always,
In all ways.
If I die trying…
At least I know
I died in love.

The Mystic Fruit

Growing out of darkness
I find myself
Carrying and withholding
Ancient Knowledge
That I need only
Be ready to have
Revealed.

I am moulded
Through the physical,
And shaped
By the mystical.

Tempt me
And I will find you...
There is no place to hide
From Truth.

And so I pray;
Let go,
Let go.

You are aware
Of what you choose—
Beneath the surface
Exists the Source.

My body is nimble,
And my sight is withheld,
Like the moon—
I can only see
One side of myself.

Soul Retrieval

For a long time,
I had been searching in the dark.
For something of meaning
A spark.

I am left with a fragmented soul
Searching for the pieces left behind.
When I face toward my past
I am reminded of my confines.

I have danced on my ashes
And slept with my bones.
Forgotten how to breathe
And find my way home.

I have howled at the moon
Praying for the Light.
To shine down
And illuminate my Night.

My Soul hears the calling
But first I must break through,
The paradigms and illusions
Of what I am convinced I knew.

I must birth myself over
Each day anew.
And trust that it is
A storm I can get through.

So let this be a mantra
To call back my wounded Soul.
I am on the journey
In search of being whole.

Dancing on your Bones

Whatever you do,
Do not turn away from your darkness.
Even when you feel you have submerged
So far deep
That you will not come back,
Do not turn a blind eye.
Face toward your shadow—
Embrace it with open arms
And a healing heart.
Call out to your soul,
And it will hear
From the distant echoes
Of your Voice
Not too far from
Where you lay.
It is darkest
Before the dawn.
You will cry,
You will scream,
You will feel like turning back
And leaving everything behind.
To cower in the shade of your
Illusory safety and security.
Allow your inner eyes
To peer in
And see what you will find.

What is struggling to surface
And appears malicious
Only longs to become a part of you
So you may know yourself more wholly.
Peel back the layers,
Peel back the veil.

And see that it is you
Who is staring back.
The you that hides behind
The mask you wear.
The forgetting of yourself
Was an agreement you have made
Long before you were here.
The tossing,
The turning,
The fussing,
The yearning.
You will experience many deaths,
But do not fear.
Remember that the shadow
Is just light
That is not yet illuminated.
Do not try to find comfort,
instead—
Bask in the moments
That you shine,
And let go lightly
Of all that comes your way.

Art

Once, I had created a masterpiece
And I know that this is true
Because, my beautiful sun,
I created this for you.

The Moon

I remember the night
That we looked at the moon
Through the bedroom window
It filled the whole room

And you began to cry saying
"Every night it's there
But we refuse to look.
It's so beautiful
It always gave but it never took."

I never did understand
What she had said that night
That made her eyes wide—
And fill with delight…

No, that night I was angry,
With God and the world.
I saw the moon through the window
And my fury unfurled

I screamed in my head
"Why must you fill my room.
Encompass my nightmares,
And remind me of my doom.

Always staring down.
Won't darkness ever come
For me to finally be able to rest.

But today, my love,
I understand
It was a test.

The moon hasn't been back
Since that one lonely night,
And now I am here
Praying for the light
Quietly.

The night unveils
And between the clouds—
A light!

Could this be my prayer answered
Despite—
My constant plea to make things right.

My lady was swept away gently
In the night
And now all I do is look up
In hope of illumination from my freight,
I never did understand what she meant
Until that dark eve

By then she had left
And nothing had been received
But quiet whispers
Encircling the room.
And shadows reminding me
Again, of my doom...
They taunt me and recall
That I once had the moon.

I Hope That You Find What You are Looking For

I hope you find
What you're looking for
In every single place
With every passing season
And through every human's face
Never lose your adventure
In the fear of losing your place
Within the world around you
this hustle, bustle and race
And I hope you never stop looking
Or find that it's a waste
For what you have experienced
Has only been a taste
Never lose yourself
Or leave the world behind
And at the end of it all
It is better to be kind
When you are in the dark
Or find your world is cold
Take time for peace
And remember, love is bold

Transfiguration

I know you feel deeply child,
I know you feel much.
Whatever you may do…
Don't close your heart.
Don't close your heart.

You may feel lost sometimes
You may feel uncertain and in the dark,
Like a flame that's been extinguished
For some time
And is searching for its spark.

I know you feel deeply, child,
I know you do feel much,
Whatever you do…
Don't close your heart.
Don't close your heart.

May the gentle breeze of the trees,
May the spirit of truth
Carry you gently through life
At least while you are here on Earth.

Starry-eyed wanderer
Seeker of truth,
Know that all you need
Is within you.
It has always been within you.

Observe the altering of the seasons,
Keep peace with your ever-changing Soul
While you are on your journey
To becoming whole.

The Unravelling

I am the universe
Experiencing itself
While the universe is also
Experiencing me

Sometimes I find myself
Anywhere
Everywhere
On the subway
Or in a beautiful forest

And I ask myself
"God, why must it be so hard?"
How can something be so beautiful?
So divine?
And make me feel so putrid?
So horrifying?
And make me feel so sick?
I find
That although I don't always
Get the answer that I am looking for
God answers
And reminds me

That I am mine
Before I am ever anyone else's
I am my first child
And I am wounded
The scars have been covered
So carefully
That I have forgotten
I hardly notice them anymore
But I always feel them.
Take the time to heal yourself.

Nobody but will understand
Except for you
And that is okay
Heal in your own way
And be your own self

Whoever
Or whatever that may be
And when you find the world
Is beating you down

And things become hard
Turn away from the outside world
And go inward
We were given two eyes to see
But only one to truly understand

Shut your eyes
And resort back to the darkness
It is not what you think
It has always been kind

The space within
Is where you may find your peace
Even if only for a moment

Let it envelope you
And remind you
That within the chaos of this life
It is the rainbow
To the everlasting storm

Become a nobody
Among the hustle and the bustle
And see
What you will find

Illuminated

Where there is dark
There will always be Light
When the night is long
The morning is bright

A fire burns in my heart,
Full of passion,
And full
Of Art.

Notice and seek around
If you are lost,
You can always
Be found.

With the bright stars above
And the Earth below.
Become a rock and you will find
That still that river will flow.

Become the river
And you will see
The river flows
Through you and me.

The Light within
Is true and kind,
Illuminate
The Soul and Mind.

Serendipity

- For Ethan

You gently washed into my life
Life soothing waves upon a shore,
And though we've met only recently
I've known you in a lifetime before…

I cherish every moment,
And when I look into your eyes,
I see an entire Universe—
In disguise.

You grace me with your kindness,
In your embrace I take shelter
And I know, like a ray shining between dark clouds
You will shine, no matter the weather.

I cherish every moment
And when I peer into your eyes,
I see an entire Soul
In disguise.

I hope one day you may realize
The beauty and light that you carry within.
With each memory made, our love deepens
And goes so much deeper than skin—

Your smile and embrace feel like home,
And balms any wound I've had before,
And I want you to know
There's no part of you I do not adore.

Grandma's Girl

"Fata lu Bunica"

I see you in my dreams sometimes,
And I feel you in my Heart.
I come to remember memories
Of my childhood spent together
Huddled, close, safe in embrace.

Thank you for your guidance,
Your presence
Your grace.
Your wisdom eternal,
The Soul beneath your eyes
And for never, never telling me lies.

I know you couldn't stay on Earth forever
But I do wish for you to know
You taught me more,
So much more than you will ever know.

In your footsteps I walked,
In your home I took haven,
I looked up to you,
I know awaken to—

Your guidance,
Your presence
Your grace.
Your wisdom eternal,
The Soul beneath your eyes
Thank you
For never, never telling me lies.

Anytime I found myself
Alone, and in the dark...
You were always there to remind me
Of the God within my Heart.
The wisdom to know
I am never alone
No matter that life is hard.

The faith that you carried
And your sweet and safe embrace,
Your words, and comforting presence...
Your philosophies, values and outlook on life.
Teaching me never to quarrel
Oh—
How it is a waste of time.

Presenting me the miracle that is existence,
How to appreciate simplicity—
A flower on the ground,
Family,
A sunset
A tree.

Thanks to you,
I know what it means to be free.
In thought, in heart, in body.
I feel now that I truly see,
Beneath the surface
Of what exists before me.

Moving Through

People will break you, child,
People will talk.
But all you've got to do
Is walk.

Walk through every moment
Walk towards the sun.
Don't let anyone tell you
You're wrong.

Life will hurt you, child
And you won't know if you can go on.
You'll be on your last limb falling
In the dark.

Nothing is as it seems,
Even the things you hold close,
But don't let them make you broken child,
Let go.

You have a life to live
So keep your head up high.
Create a vision
And fly.

Tomorrow is for the taking,
and yesterday is tossed...
The present is in clear view
but you are lost.

The storm may leave you heavy,
And your mistakes are close behind.
Whatever you do,
be kind.

Life will do whatever it can
To close your heart.
Just keep breathing,
It's hard.

You are all you have
In truth, you are always alone.
So just keep moving—
Make room for love to grow.

The Wild Self

I am but a
Withered child,
Running through
The open wild.
Earth below me,
Sky above—
Learning what
It is to love.

Light

If I could give my Self
A few words of advice
It would be to live Light,
And to be the Light.
To hold on,
And to have the wisdom
To know
When to let go.
To stay rooted,
And allow the Flow.

Libertas Perfundet Omnia Luce
"Freedom will flood all things with light."

What's in your heart, child?
What's in your heart?
What is it
That creates your spark?

What makes you feel free?
What brings your closer
To infinity?

What makes you bleed child,
From the inside out?
What do you fear, child?
When you look out into the world?
What is buried,
Deep in your Soul?

Breathe, child, breathe.
You were made to fly.
Cast out all your ashes
Up into the sky.

Let the world come in, child.
Do not be afraid.
It is only your mind,
That exists within a cage.

You are my Sun

You are my sun
who radiates beautiful white light
and nourishes my body and soul

When you look at me
I know
you are there,
you are listening

You notice every little crevice,
every detail of my speech and body—
and I the same

When we lay together...
your comforting warmth
helps me to find stillness and peace

And I feel so much,
even when you are gone
or drifting away

There is always so much more I can do or say
I hope that you are happy
where you are right now in this moment

Asleep, and exploring
the realm of your inner being
I am always right there with you

The Voice Within

God answers prayers
In the quiet miracles
Of everyday living.

Unconditional Love

I asked my Self
What do I do
With all of this Love?

"Spread it like wildfire,
And tend to the flame,
By feeding it every day.
Nurture your body,
Your mind,
And your Soul.
Allow the Light to enter
And brighten your being.
So, always
Choose Love.
Be careful
Not to hold on too tightly—
Love is nourished and embraced
Through space and movement.
It requires growth,
Patience,
Wisdom,
And above all
Truth."

Ode to Wild Woman

If you wish
For your woman
To stay wild
And you pride
In seeing her free,
Be gentle...
And strong.
Shine alongside her.
Give her room,
And always,
Always know
That the gates of her Heart
Remain open to you.
Be patient...
Be kind.
She will hold a deep love
For you
That will
Shine bright enough
To withstand all the dark
Of the night sky—
All the storms
To come;
The deep vast oceans
And waves.
She will honour you,
As she honours herself
And all of creation.

Stay Wild

I've come to learn a few things
Of which I know to be true.
It's good to enjoy the simple life—
Family and friends too.

When times get hard,
And when you feel alone...
Know that within your Soul
Exists a Light to guide you home.

I've come to learn a few things,
Of this I know to be true.
Stay humble and wise,
These virtues are far and few.

Kindred animal spirits and plants,
The forests and the trees...
Exists and may remind you
That humans are intrinsically at ease.

So, may you find peace of mind
Wherever you may be.
Though I pray,
Cultivate eyes that see—

The beauty of others,
The possibilities.
That happiness does not lie in wealth,
But in moments and memories.
I hope that you may cultivate,
A spirit that is free.

Love Letters to the Universe

Where do all these thoughts come from?
And where will they all go?
From within the ashes that will eventually come,
Will various flowers grow?
Will I become a part of the tide?
That will carry me to the sea,
Do I stand to reside
With the Soul that exists within me?
I ask these questions,
In hopes that one day I will understand
The vast interconnected nature
Between humans and the land
You see,
I may not be much of a talker
But I have a lot to say
I continue to ask questions...
Everyday.
Will I become a part of the tide
That will carry me to the sea,
Do I stand to reside
With the Soul that exists within me?
See, from when I was a child,
I had a joy in my heart
When connecting—
With an animal, nature
Or Art.
There are days when I awaken,
And I know the light that exists within me,
Which has carried me on my journeys,
From Europe to the mountains of Costa Rica and BC...
And so,
I ask these questions,
In hopes that one day I may know

Where do we come from?
Where will we go?
Will we become a part of the Earth
That has nurtured us tenderly,
Or will we return into the Cosmos
The heavenly stars, the primordial energy?

Solace

Let my body rot,
Where flowers can now grow—
May it be so,
May it be so

Rid me of this body
Where only illusions flow…
My canvas has never been there
It has always been my Soul

Water may run through me
Like blood into my veins…
Let me crumble like soil,
Never to be seen again

Infinite Possibilities

What is on the inside
Looking out, I say?
Memories, thoughts
And dreams left astray?
What is on the inside
Looking out?
A beam of infinite light
Or a Soul left to decay?
Unwritten poetry
Or a mind that's in a haze?
Who is on the inside
Looking out…
And are they
Here to stay?

Paint

Blank canvas, blank space
Empty state of mind
Suddenly paint appears
And at once I begin to think
"It is so beautiful without anything
So clear and so bright
But weren't they made
To be painted on?"
Vibrant yellow and deep blues
An emotional swirl
In an instance
Realizations
Am I the painter
Or it which shall be created?
I began to press
Just one finger
Against the empty space
A line of green
"It is merely a line,
But it changed the whole view
Is there any more
That I can do?"
Dipping my finger in the blue
I begin to draw waves
"This is for the anchor that lays
Between my breasts,
The wretched melancholy
That always finds its way back"
And the waves become more and more violent
Until they cover half of the canvas
"What have I done?
This is not what I intended
I let myself

Get carried away by the sea"
Bringing myself back to shore
I draw back and see what I've done
I begin to place multiple fingers
In an array of colours
Indigos, browns, reds and others
Until I find that every finger
is a different colour

I smear the paint across the canvas
From the very top
To the smallest corners
Until there are no white spots left
And I realize the canvas is a multitude
Of different combinations
And mixtures
Some areas are grey
From too much layering
Others are clean and pure

"I shall let
This canvas represent the falters of my life
And the achievements
The sadness
And the joy
The moments of insight
And the grey and dull apathy
Everything under the sun"
Grabbing at the corner
I begin to peel away at the paint
That I had invested time in creating
To find a blank canvas once again
A masterpiece

"Peel away at yourself
And you will find that behind it all,
It is blank
And the root of truth lies there"

The sun was shining down
On the blank slate
I began to look at my skin
And began peeling away
Until I found that all that was left
Was light
Pure white light
"This is my canvas"
I whispered
And
Instantly disappeared

Acceptance

Dance your rhythm
In the shoes of those who have died
Do not fear—
Fear is the enemy of the brave.
Laugh,
Laugh until you can see
The silhouette of your breath
Rise up into
The crisp autumn air
Laugh in the face of death
It is when you are not.

Ephemeral

In you,
I find my will,
and through you—
I find strength

You shine through,
On dark days
Your rays, penetrate
through impenetrable haze,
Though I know not where
I seek you

I rebuild using
The ashes of
What I have sown,
A home—
The same one I held dear
The one I had once known

Full of vision,
Memories,
and dreams once recalled…
I wander now,
Through this empty hall
In search of you

Horizon

I can see it, now
The illuminating light
Vast and distant
Which fills the night
I can see it, now

For many years
I've roamed the lonely sea
In search of what
Exists before me—
A hopeful horizon

I beg, and plead
And I implore that
This turbulent sea
May lead to
Evermore

I can see it, now
The illuminating light
Vast and distant
Which fills the night
I can see it, now

In search of meaning, and
With a need to explore
I venture off
Into the ineffable
Where I may soar

Letting Go

Vivid colours
Vivid smoke
Like paint on a canvas
Each day, a stroke

I wish
I could just
Hold on
A little bit longer

Ashes to darkness
Darkness to Light
Everything in between
Emerging so bright—

Joy and grief,
Anger and strife
The darkness and ashes
Turns to Light

Finding myself
Somewhere inclined
Each day, a mountain
For me to climb, and yet

I wish
I could just
Hold on
A little bit longer

I Found, You

After the long nights wondering
The days spent in a haze
I found, you
You—
With your inner fire set ablaze

Beside you, I seize
The moments and the days
Beside you, I wake
And to the thought of you
I drift off into the night with,
Everyday

After the long nights wondering
The days spent in haze
With your light, joy and laughter
Your soul set ablaze
You appear before me

Light, joy and love embodied
And our first meeting, fateful
With the morning sun,
I pray for you—
I am grateful,
I am grateful.

Meaningful Meanderings

Voices of people,
Figments of grace
Chasing ecstasy, time
In what seems, a race

In search of what?
And what for?
I know but this,
Strive for more

I gaze within
A spacious void
Of dreams once planted
And thoughts deployed

And I know not how
Or for what I am here—
Allow me this
'fore I disappear:

Like the sun
May you rise
Like the moon
May you fall

Find your solace
Clasp your grace
And remain soft
Through it all

Allow none
To steal your light
And throughout it all
Continue to fight

Though the dual path
May be darkly lit
You will find your self—
Luminous and moonlit

Full Moon Risin'

Rays shine across
Golden fields and
Hills of green
Where I reminisce—
On forgotten dreams

Inaudible laughter and
Church bells chime
Reminding me of
Another time,
Long ago—

A distant home,
My saving grace…
My garden of Eden
A green grove,
Timeless and still

Happiness

I have recently discovered that
Happiness does not
Come from being still
But instead from constantly moving
And keeping your heart focused
On the simple things
And most importantly
Being okay to be alone
Because you will often find
You were never alone
At all

Acknowledgements

To my family and friends for the sweet support and nurture they have provided throughout the years.

To my beautiful love who lights up my life and inspires me everyday.

And to the Creator—
May all Hearts beat as one.

 Codrina Ibanescu is a Toronto-based poet, photographer and environmentalist. Dedicated to enriching the lives of others, the environment, and with a deep reverence for the arts, she finds her deepest form of creative expression ultimately remains in her writing.